LONG HIGH SCHOOL SPORTS

LONG ISLAND HIGH SCHOOL SPORTS

Christopher R. Vaccaro

ARCADIA
PUBLISHING

Published by Arcadia Publishing
Charleston SC, Chicago IL, Portsmouth NH, San Francisco CA

Printed in the United States of America

Library of Congress Control Number: 2009923307

For all general information contact Arcadia Publishing at:
Telephone 843-853-2070
Fax 843-853-0044
E-mail sales@arcadiapublishing.com
For customer service and orders:
Toll-Free 1-888-313-2665

Visit us on the Internet at www.arcadiapublishing.com

To the coaches and athletes who have made Long Island

high school sports what they are today

CONTENTS

ACKNOWLEDGMENTS

Many people were helpful in giving me photographs to help bridge the gap of Long Island's high school sports history. They are (in no specific order) the Suffolk County Sports Hall of Fame, the Bridgehampton Historical Society, the East Hampton Historical Society, Riverhead High School athletic director Bill Groth, Southampton High School athletic director Darren Phillips, Hank Bjorklund, Garden City historian John Ellis Kordes, Garden City High School sports historian Jack White, Westhampton Beach High School athletic director Kathy Masterson, Bellport High School football coach Joe Cipp, Friends Academy, former Chaminade High School football coach Bill Basel, Huntington High School historian Jack Abrams, Baldwin High School football coach Steve Carroll, Hempstead's Albie Douglas, former Amityville High School football coach Lou Howard, the Central Islip High School football booster club, Islip High School athletic director Bob Panariello, Bay Shore High School athletic director Judy Cummings, Hauppauge High School athletic director Joe Tasman, Frank Patti, Sachem High School football, former Sachem High School wrestling coach Jack Mahoney, Bayport High School athletic director Tim Mullins, town of Brookhaven historian Barbara Russell, Joe Jay Jalbert, Richard Rewkowski, Mempham High School wrestling coach Rich Anderson, Bill Brennan and the Friends of Long Island Wrestling, former Manhasset High School lacrosse coach Alan Lowe, current Manhasset lacrosse and football coach Bill Cherry, former Garden City lacrosse assistant Doug Dwyer, Dana Kaplan, Kings Park High School athletic director Ken Ferrazzi, Shoreham Wading River High School girls' lacrosse coach Rob Vlahakis, former Lynbrook High School baseball coach Don Roth, former Sachem High School lacrosse coach Rick Mercurio, East Rockaway High School historian Joe Lores, East Islip High School, Carle Place High School, Brett Mauser, former Farmingdale High School football coach Don Snyder, Ward Melville High School, the San Diego Chargers, the Chicago Machine, the Houston Texans, the Buffalo Bills, the Miami Dolphins, the Baltimore Ravens, the Washington Nationals, the Indianapolis Colts, the Chicago White Sox, the United States Naval Academy, Purdue University, Georgia Tech, St. Joseph's College (Long Island), Yale University, the University of North Carolina, Southern Methodist University, the University of Louisville, Davidson College, the University of Virginia, Duquesne University, Penn State University, the University of Tennessee, Hofstra University, the University of Notre Dame, the University of Pittsburgh, Stanford University, C. W. Post, the Ohio State University, Manhattan College, Duke University, Rutgers University, the University of Massachusetts, Johns Hopkins University, Georgetown University, Roanoke College, Boston College, Yankton College, Clemson University, and Miami University (Ohio).

Thanks to Arcadia Publishing for helping bring this historic collection to fruition. The company produces beautiful books and is helping restore history with every book it publishes.

Without the gifted and talented teams, coaches, programs, players, and supporters, this history would have never happened.

Finally, I thank my family and friends for their support. Without them, I am nothing.

INTRODUCTION

For many years, Native Americans were the only residents of Long Island. The first recorded encounter of Europeans and the natives was in 1524 when Giovanni da Verrazano sailed into New York Bay. He did not know it then, but Verrazano stumbled upon a ripe land, with a bright future, soon to be filled with history from all walks of life.

Dutch settlers began taking control of the eastern portion of the island in 1640, and all of Long Island was under English dominion by 1664. The English developed Kings, Queens, and Suffolk Counties in 1683, and although Nassau County took up 70 percent of Queens County, it was not officially named Nassau until 1899.

Through those changes grew educational systems, schools, neighborhoods, and town development.

High school sports on Long Island have existed since 1884, when the now defunct St. Paul's School of Garden City fielded a football team. Since then, thousands of games have been played, athletes have become professional stars, youngsters have become men and women, and Long Island has garnered its fair share of historic lore on the sports field.

While Brooklyn and Queens are located on the 118-mile stretch of land that makes up America's biggest island, this book encompasses the pictorial history of athletics from Nassau and Suffolk Counties. A large percentage of the schools in each county belong to the New York State Public High School Athletic Association, and more importantly most, if not all, sports have a Long Island championship, making for some outstanding competitive games all school year long.

Within two decades of St. Paul's first athletic programs, many other schools across Long Island were developing, both as academic and athletic institutions. Friends Academy in Locust Valley already had football in 1895, Riverhead High School had track-and-field teams in the late 1890s, Southampton High School had football in 1903, Huntington High School had football in 1897, and others like Freeport, Greenport, and East Hampton started following suit quickly after.

In total, there are 57 public schools in Nassau (Section VIII) and 61 in Suffolk (Section XI). There are about 15 others on the island that participate in the Catholic High School Athletic Association or private school leagues.

With this amount of schools and athletes flooding the area comes a rich tradition of athletic history. Turn any random sports game on television and in some way there is a Long Island connection. Many hall of famers were nurtured in Nassau and Suffolk Counties, including Jim Brown (Manhasset), Julius Irving (Roosevelt), and Carl Yastrzemski (Bridgehampton). Other stars include Craig Biggio (Kings Park), Boomer Esiason (East Islip), Vinny Testaverde (Sewanhaka), and Larry Brown (Long Beach).

Among the island's most notable sports is lacrosse, which the area has become a hotbed for. Lacrosse players from Long Island are recruited annually by the nation's top colleges and universities, often winning championships, leading the NCAA in statistical categories and eventually finding their way to professional lacrosse leagues. Although the sport was not played on Long Island until the 1930s, it picked up drastically, and the island has developed an outstanding reputation as a result. The nation's longest uninterrupted high school lacrosse rivalry is the battle between Garden City and Manhasset—dubbed the Woodstick Classic—which dates back to 1935 and features some of the best players in the nation every year.

Manhasset was the first school to develop a lacrosse program. As early as 1931, young student athletes were using the old basket weave sticks to toss passes and take shots. Garden City and Friends Academy joined the picture in 1931, Sewanhaka in 1938, and in 1957, Huntington became the first Suffolk County school to have a team.

Although not like Florida, Texas, or California in its skill level, football on Long Island has a strong following. It is probably the sport that is most cared about by residents, sports fans, and athletes. Thousands watch the Long Island championships every year at Stony Brook University's Kenneth P. LaValle Stadium and Hofstra University's James M. Shuart Stadium. There have been major players in every decade from Lawrence's Ray Barbuti in the 1920s, who still holds some Nassau County records, to Manhasset's Brown in the 1950s, Esiason at East Islip in the 1970s, and North Babylon's Jason Gwaltney in the first decade of the 21st century.

In the early days, the backbone of Long Island was fishing and farming. It was very common for teams to play on the potato farms on the east end. It was not until the 1920s and 1930s that Long Island made the transition from a rural area to the classic American suburb. The population grew drastically after World War II, which meant the development of better and larger school systems, thus leading to high school sports teams.

Today there are nine professional sports organizations that play on Long Island, from the New York Mets, New York Islanders, Long Island Rough Riders (soccer), Long Island Lizards (lacrosse), and New York Titans (lacrosse) to the Long Island Ducks (baseball), Brooklyn Cyclones (baseball), Strong Island Sound (basketball), and the New York Dragons (arena football, but the league is in a financial crisis). The first black baseball team, the New York Cuban Giants, was formed in Babylon in 1885. World Series and Stanley Cups have been won on the island; professional football teams have played games and practiced there; presidents, artists, authors, movie stars, and luminaries of all kinds have come and gone; but through it all, high school sports have stayed and left a mark.

In this book you will find pictures from almost every school and every major program. Each chapter lists photographs in chronological order. If you are wondering why a team, school, or certain athlete or coach is not in the book there is a simple answer: it was not obtainable. Thousands of calls, e-mails, and faxes were made to athletic directors, coaches, and historical societies over several months to gather photographs for this project. Not every major figure in Long Island history—there are thousands—could possibly fit in this. Instead, there is an eclectic collection of photographs from various sports and schools. Gathering these photographs, many of which came from closets and attics and have not been touched for decades, was a pleasure and an important linkage of history on Long Island.

1

GRIDIRON GLORY

FA, stitched on the chest of the young man's sweater on the bottom left, is the marking of Friends Academy in Locust Valley. This is its 1895 football team and one of the oldest group photographs of any team in Long Island history. From left to right in the first row are Lou Rushmore, Ed Downing, Ed Underhill, and Charlie Vail. In the second row, in no particular order, are Clarence Chamberlin, Henry Dudger, Jacob Seaman, Cary Burlis, James Stewart, James Willets, Charles Wharton, William Miller, Gilbert Hall, and Charles Wyong. (Friends Academy.)

This is the oldest known football photograph from Southampton High School. The 1904 football team is a gangly bunch, filled with characters sporting long eyebrows, bow ties, strange curly hair, and one guy with his jock around his neck. Based on the photograph, it looks like the beige or white sweaters most of the boys are wearing served as their main uniform. Their pants, with ribbed pads on the thighs for protection, are as old school as one will see. (Southampton High School.)

There were no major awards given out for high school football on Long Island in the 1920s. There were titles and a few competitive teams. This is the 1924 Riverhead High School football team. Sporting their stripe-sleeved Riverhead jersey sweaters are coach Martin and his gang. Among those pictured are F. Creighton, A. Bobinski, G. Cooper, C. F. Hallett, C. Bobinski, G. Stivers, coach Martin, N. Corwin, W. Sanford, M. McCabe, S. Franzik, and team manager W. S. Conklin. (Riverhead High School.)

Ray Barbuti still holds some Nassau County rushing records from his days at Lawrence High School. In 1923, Barbuti scored 48 points and 8 touchdowns in a game against Southampton. Some say he may have scored nine touchdowns that day, which would tie the current Long Island record. He is also credited with a Long Island record 102-yard touchdown run in the Southampton game. This picture shows Barbuti rushing the ball for Syracuse University in 1926 against Colgate. (Patti family.)

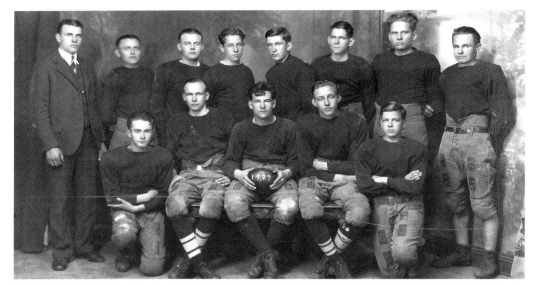

Football started in Bay Shore in 1927 with this group of strapping young Long Island natives. The Maroon lost its first game 32-0 to Patchogue and went 0-4 in the inaugural season. From left to right are (first row) Fred Wicks, Sam Widdifield, Ed Flynn (captain), Burt Leyrer, and George Brown; (second row) coach Clifton A. LaPlatney, Max Strehlau, Ray Jarvis, Wilmot Wiley, Cornelius Linehan, Paul Cronin, "Guts" Guttinger, and Louis Mass. (Bay Shore High School.)

The Bonackers of East Hampton High School had some interesting uniforms in the 1930s with a large letter *E* on their chests. This 1931 team had a number of players, but their names are all unknown. Most Suffolk County high school records before 1945 are very fuzzy, so without a sticker or plate on the photograph to say how this specific team did, it is hard to know how successful it was. (East Hampton Library, Long Island Collection.)

GRIDIRON GLORY

Although not the clearest photograph, this is one of the oldest from both Baldwin High School's and Hempstead High School's football programs. Taken during a game in 1934 that was played at Altoona Field, where the current Hempstead Middle School is situated, the photograph shows large crowds and vintage stripped jerseys. (Steve Carroll, Baldwin High School.)

This is a Baldwin-Freeport game in 1936. Called "Election Day Madness" because of the quality of the football between the two towns and because of the large attendance by community members on Election Day, the Baldwin-Freeport football game was truly a sporting spectacle every year. Baldwin won this game 12-7 and went 8-1 that year, winning the Nassau County championship. (Steve Carroll, Baldwin High School.)

It was not rare to find Baldwin High School playing schools from all over the country in the 1930s. Here in 1936, Bill Dunphy from White Plains is rushing the ball past No. 25 Alley Clark and No. 22 John Fitzgerald. Baldwin won the game 19-13. According to Baldwin football coach Steve Carroll, White Plains is wearing black and orange jerseys and Baldwin left early in the morning to take a bus trip for the road game. (Steve Carroll, Baldwin High School.)

Baldwin and Petersburg, Virginia, the best team in the South during the 1930s, squared off four times from 1934 to 1938. This photograph is from the final game of the series in 1938, a 14-0 win for Petersburg. Steve Carroll's uncle Edwin Orgass is the quarterback in the single wing offense about to get crushed by Petersburg's line. Petersburg won the all-time series 2-1-1. (Steve Carroll, Baldwin High School.)

GRIDIRON GLORY

This picture of Baldwin High School football is from the 1940s and was taken at Gardiner's Field. According to Carroll that was one of the first fields around with a field house. The flags behind No. 18 are positioned where the main entrance to the stadium was. Carroll believes the picture must be from after World War II because the flags went up around the time an alumni game was played to raise money for veterans from the war. (Steve Carroll, Baldwin High School.)

Fans drenched the sidelines during every Baldwin-Freeport football game. While the games still have a big impact on fans today, these games from the 1940s had people standing on houses that wrapped around the old Freeport Race Track, which was used up until the mid-1980s. In this photograph, from the 1940s, notice the referees, who look like milk men, and the yard marker signs written on the wall of the track. (Steve Carroll, Baldwin High School.)

The 1940 Garden City football team scrimmages against St. Paul's School in this photograph. According to Garden City sports historian Jack White, Long Island's first high school football game was played between St. Paul's and Poly Prep in 1884. (Jack White, Garden City High School.)

This group of Amityville football players was part of the 1940 varsity team that went undefeated and untied. To the left is head coach Homer Ball, who finished his coaching career with 96 victories, which puts him in the top 15 for Suffolk County's all-time wins list. In the No. 30 jersey is Lou Howard, who would eventually go on to coach at Amityville and have as much success, if not more, than Ball at the helm of the program. (Lou Howard.)

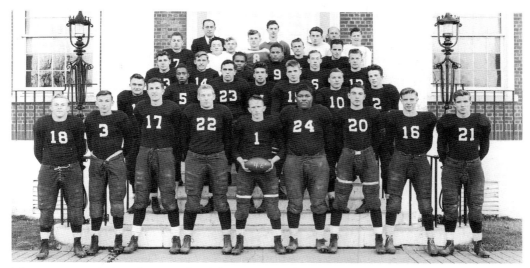

The mat around this photograph of the 1947 Southampton football team shows that it won the Suffolk County championship and the score of every game in its perfect 7-0 season. The Mariners beat Amityville 20-0 in the championship. They also opened the season with a 20-14 win over Oceanside, blanked Malverne 21-0, and destroyed Greenport 47-0. The Mariners beat local rival Westhampton 33-13 and East Hampton 32-6. They finished the regular season with a 19-12 win over Riverhead. (Southampton High School.)

Not much is known about Bill McGarry except that this photograph from 1949 had "outstanding runner" written on the bottom of it. In a time when action photography was not too prevalent in high school sports, McGarry was captured in all his running glory as a running back at Chaminade High School. The old school long-sleeve jersey and leather helmet show how the equipment of the time was far different than today. (Chaminade High School.)

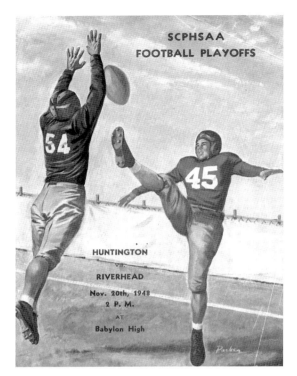

This program is from the 1948 Suffolk County football championship game between Huntington High School and Riverhead High School, held at Babylon High School on November 20. Huntington beat Riverhead 26-14 to capture the title. The Blue Devils went on to beat Greenport the following season 27-0. (Huntington High School.)

Huntington won 71 out of 126 games under the guidance of coach Bill Class. He coached the school to the 1948 Suffolk County football championship game. Riverhead won titles in 1936, 1939, and 1941, and both schools had dominant seasons heading into this game. The Blue Devils won their first boys' basketball title the year before. (Huntington High School.)

This organized bunch is the 1954 Westhampton Beach High School football team. This team was coached by Carl Hansen (second from right), who is a legend and the namesake for the football field in Westhampton Beach. The award given to Suffolk County's most outstanding football player each year is named after him. (Westhampton Beach High School.)

The 1955 Chaminade High School football team went 2-4-1. The program, which started in 1930, has had a long-standing history in the Catholic High School Athletic Association. For the last quarter century, the Flyers have built a rivalry with South Huntington's St. Anthony's High School that is hard to top, especially on the football and lacrosse fields. Chaminade won its first title in 1956. (Chaminade High School.)

Bernie Wyatt may be the best athlete in Amityville history. In this photograph from 1956, Wyatt is scrambling on a famous run to break Jim Brown's Long Island scoring record of 170 points in eight games. Wyatt went on to the University of Iowa, was team MVP in 1960, was selected in the 19th round of the 1961 NFL draft by the Pittsburgh Steelers, and eventually became an assistant coach at Iowa and later the University of Wisconsin. (Lou Howard.)

Howie Vogts, who is the winningest coach in New York state football history with more than 340 victories and was still coaching when this book was printed, is standing to the left of his team in this 1956 photograph. This particular Bethpage team went 6-0-2 in the school's fifth overall season. (Richard Rewkowski.)

This random action shot from the 1950s shows Friends Academy on the defensive side of a football game, making a tackle. More importantly, look at the face masks of the players. The helmet structure is very similar to what regular helmets were throughout the next 50 years, but the face mask is very unstable. Most historical data on older football helmets show at least a modified plastic face piece during that time period. That little cloth addition is very rare. (Friends Academy.)

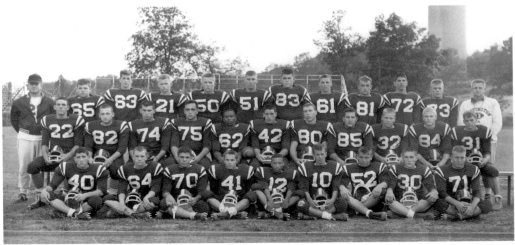

This picture may be popular for one reason only. Aside from featuring former Huntington High School football coach Al Donofrio (far left), it depicts a younger Fred Fusaro (third from left on the bottom) during his junior year at Huntington. Fusaro went on to coach at Sachem High School. Also in the photograph in the first row (No. 52) is Paul Hackett, one of Fusaro's assistant coaches at Sachem. (Huntington High School.)

At Lawrence High School, Sal Ciampi was a bruiser. He helped lead the 1961 team to the Rutgers Cup and a Nassau County title over Hempstead High School. Ciampi, pictured here in his Purdue University uniform, won the Thorp Award as Nassau's best player and left to play at Purdue. He was a three-year starter and is ranked as the best player in Purdue history to ever wear No. 68. He went on to coach baseball and football at East Islip High School and is a legend in both avenues. (Purdue University.)

Don McCauley, Garden City's best football player ever, rushes the ball in 1966 for the Trojans. He went to the University of North Carolina and led the nation in rushing (1,720) and all-purpose yards (2,021) in 1970. In 1971, he was the Atlantic Coast Conference Athlete of the Year and was selected by the Baltimore Colts in the first round of the NFL draft (22nd overall). A member of the College Football Hall of Fame, McCauley became one of the NFL's premier third-down specialists at a time when that role was very limited. (Jack White, Garden City High School.)

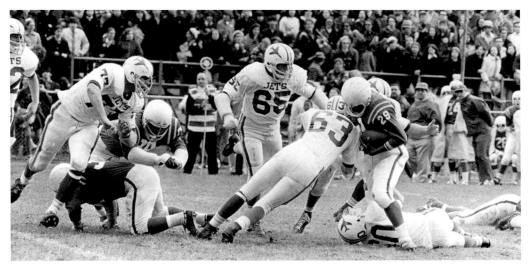

Lawrence running back Mike Spikes is trying to plow through East Meadow guard Mike Schmalz (No. 63). Tony Schmidt (No. 65) stands close to the action during the game that took place on October 26, 1968. East Meadow did not win its first Nassau County title on the gridiron until 2006 when the Jets beat Freeport 35-34 in the Conference I championship game. It lost to William Floyd 42-20 in the Class I Long Island championship the following week. (East Meadow High School.)

As one of the purest athletes of his time, Tom Black set himself apart on the football and baseball fields at Central Islip High School. He was offered a contract by the San Francisco Giants after he graduated but opted to attend East Texas State on a football scholarship and eventually became an All-American. The San Francisco 49ers took him in the 14th round of the 1969 NFL draft, but a knee injury prevented him from playing. (Suffolk County Sports Hall of Fame.)

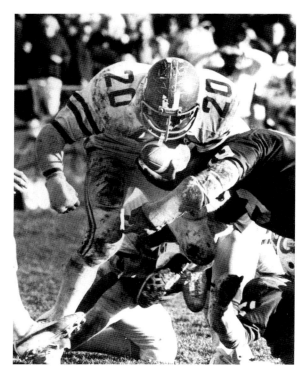

Rodney Cooke was Bellport's first Hansen Award winner. In 1980, Cooke was All-League, All-County, All-Long Island, and a first-team All-State selection. He played fullback and linebacker for coach Joe Cipp. He helped pave the way for strong backs in Bellport, which won its first Suffolk County title in 1982, a 42-6 win over Sayville. (Joe Cipp, Bellport High School.)

Tom Watson was Bellport's second Hansen winner. The offensive and defensive end was an All-League, All-County, and All-Long Island selection. He was fourth-team All-State and led the Clippers with six fumble recoveries and 11 quarterback sacks in 1982. (Joe Cipp, Bellport High School.)

Antonio O'Ferral graduated from Bellport in 1990 and had one of the best careers of any Clipper ever. He played at the University of Kentucky and left with the Bellport record in passing yards (2,303). His 1,603 yards of total offense in 1989 pushed him to one of the best seasons in school history as well. (Joe Cipp, Bellport High School.)

In 1990, Bethpage beat New Hyde Park 42-6 to win the Nassau County Conference III title. This was before any Long Island championships were played. Notice the 2:00 on the scoreboard in between the score. This marked the 200th win in Howie Vogts's very long coaching career. (Richard Rewkowski.)

The Seattle Seahawks selected Central Islip's Eric Unverzagt (class of 1991) with their fourth-round pick (131st overall) in the 1996 NFL draft. Unverzagt, who is an assistant coach at Central Islip now, went to the University of Wisconsin and played two seasons with the Seahawks on defense. This picture, although it is hard to tell, features a bloody Unverzagt during his high school playing days. (Central Islip High School Football Booster Club.)

Seen here is 1st. Lt. Ron Winchester, a member of the 1st Battalion, 7th Marine Regiment based in Twentypine Palms, California. At 25 years old Winchester died in Anbar province, Iraq, in September 2004. Winchester graduated from the United States Naval Academy in 2001 where he played football. He played lacrosse and football at Chaminade High School. (United States Naval Academy.)

At St. Anthony's High School, Joe Villani lettered four times in football, twice in lacrosse, and once in basketball. He led the Friars to the 2001 Catholic High School Football League championship and was selected to New York's Golden 50 as one of the top high school players in the state. As a walk-on, Villani made the roster at the University of Pittsburgh and rose to be a starter in 2005 at the center position. (University of Pittsburgh.)

By the time Alex Fletcher reached his senior season at Stanford University, he was one of the Pac-10's top offensive linemen. The center started almost every game he played during his collegiate career and signed with the New Orleans Saints in April 2009. The St. Anthony's High School graduate was an Elite 50 selection and consensus All-American. (Stanford University.)

Ed Gowins was a pure back. He was solid and fast and had great field vision. He was the 2006 Hansen Award winner and was All-Long Island, All-Suffolk, and All-Division his senior year, in which he rushed for 1,996 yards and 34 touchdowns. The Clippers were 21-1 in his final two seasons before he went on to the Bridgeton Academy in Maine and eventually Stony Brook University. (Christopher R. Vaccaro.)

Bellport honored those lost in the attacks of 9/11 by wearing FDNY hats after its 42-19 win over Southside in the Class II Long Island title game. Bellport's Mike McPartland's father, Mike, is an FDNY battalion chief for the 11th Battalion. Joe Cipp asked McPartland to represent the FDNY at the game. (Joe Cipp, Bellport High School.)

North Babylon literally ran away with the show when Jason Gwaltney was on the team. He was a bruising running back who put up numbers in the record books that will certainly never be broken. Gwaltney was the first player to ever win back-to-back Hansen Awards (2003–2004) and lit the record books up. He finished his career with many Long Island records, including 7,800 career rushing yards, and owns the single-season record with 2,882 yards in 2004. (C. W. Post.)

In 2008, Terrell Williams became the sixth Hempstead High School football player to win the Thorp Award. He finished his Tigers career with the most all-purpose yards (4,799), touchdowns (42), and points (266) in school history. During his senior season, he had 1,379 rushing yards and 23 total touchdowns. (Albie Douglas.)

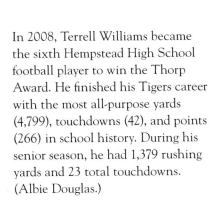

In their second of three straight Long Island title games, the 2006 William Floyd football team beat East Meadow 42-20 at Hofstra University's James M. Shuart Stadium. Putting together a string of 42 straight wins that was snapped in 2008, the Colonials went undefeated in 2006 and won their second of three consecutive Rutgers Trophies that season as well. (Christopher R. Vaccaro.)

Brock Jackolski of the William Floyd High School football squad was the best high school football player Long Island may ever have. He led the Colonials to a 33-0 mark and three straight Long Island, Suffolk County, and Division I titles, won the 2007 Hansen Award as Suffolk County's top player, and was named New York State Player of the Year for Class AA his senior season. The lightning-quick back was also a defensive back and kick returner and went on to play at Hofstra University. He rushed for 3,603 yards and 64 touchdowns in high school. (Hofstra University.)

GRIDIRON GLORY

2

HOOPS GALORE

In one of the oldest photographs of an organized girls' basketball team on Long Island, the 1897 Friends Academy team poses for the camera. Sporting FA jerseys and all-black uniforms, the team, which is large in number for a sport that only needs five at a time on the court, was a pioneer in girls' basketball on Long Island. (Friends Academy.)

Many teams at St. Paul's played some freshman college programs from New York City. The 1906 basketball team played Columbia and lost 14-13. The team went 4-6 that season and the score of its game against Dwight on January 19 is unknown. This team consisted of ? Woodruff (captain), John Patton, H. V. Seggerman, Noah Nason, William Blandy, A. John, R. E. Biggs, and J. M. Hartwell. (Garden City Archives.)

Mrs. Howard Downs donated this photograph to Riverhead High School many years after it was taken in 1909. Downs must have been a relative of Althea Downs, who is second from the left. On the far left is Ethel Sullivan, and following Downs are Maude Burgess, Anna Garvey, and Alice Hallock. Aside from the high hair, they all have dresses for jerseys. (Riverhead High School.)

The 1910 Huntington High School boys' basketball program is one of the first in school history. On a very old index card that accompanied the photograph at the high school's archives, it says "second team." This probably means it was the second team in school history after the 1909 one, which was coached by a Mr. Latham. (Huntington High School.)

This poorly dressed 1912 Friends Academy basketball team consists of, from left to right, Russell Peltict, Bill Waysmith, Aaron Hallock, Valentine Wills, ? Botsford, Bob Bills, and Howard Petit. Although Friends Academy was lacking in competitive spirit for most of the 20th century, the 2004–2005 team won the Class C Long Island championship. (Friends Academy.)

Coach Harold A. Carroll put together what was known as "the Wonder Team" for the 1921–1922 season at Bay Shore High School. The Maroon went 22-3 this season, outscored its opponents 653-346, and beat Westhampton Beach 36-17 and 44-19 in a two-game series to capture the school's first Suffolk County championship. Bay Shore went on to beat Nassau County's Lawrence High School 46-25 in the Long Island title game. (Bay Shore High School.)

This picture of the 1924–1925 Islip girls' varsity basketball team was donated to Islip High School by a family member of Mary Koncelik, who is standing in the top row, second from the right. They most likely won the Suffolk County championship based on the word *champs* written on the ball and by the rather small trophy being held by the young lady in the center. (Islip High School.)

By 1927, the New York State Public High School Athletic Association had held six annual state basketball tournaments. This particular year's tournament was held in Buffalo in late March. It is unknown who won the New York State title, but Southampton High School, where this program was found, did win the Suffolk County and Long Island boys' titles that year. (Southampton High School.)

NEW YORK STATE
PUBLIC HIGH SCHOOL
ATHLETIC ASSOCIATION

SIXTH ANNUAL STATE CHAMPIONSHIP
BASKET BALL TOURNAMENT

BROADWAY AUDITORIUM
BUFFALO, N. Y.

THURSDAY - FRIDAY - SATURDAY
MARCH 24, 25 and 26
1927

As can be seen, Islip had warm-up sweatshirts for its basketball team. The Buccaneers were runners-up in the Suffolk County championship in 1929. From left to right are (first row) Robert Berry, Herbert Muncey, and Walter Morris; (second row) Bill Weber, Frank Sindler, James Egan, and Frank Macik; (third row) head coach Lawrence Lobaugh, William Golden, Earl Robinson, and Franklin Whitman. (Islip High School.)

The East Hampton Library's Long Island room dug this old photograph of the 1930 East Hampton High School girls' basketball team out of its archives. Since there were few schools on the island with proper transportation to bring teams around, some believe many teams traveled via train, especially those heading east from parts of western Suffolk County and Nassau County. (East Hampton Library, Long Island Collection)

The only recognizable names from this photograph of the 1930 Huntington High School boys' basketball team are captain William Freidank, coach Class, and team manager Richard Allan, as written on an index card attached to the original photograph. The team supposedly finished third place in the western Suffolk County Class A league. (Huntington High School.)

This early photograph of the Huntington boys' basketball team, taken by photographer J. V. Feather, appeared in the *Brooklyn Daily Eagle* newspaper. Among those pictured are John Burne, team captain Claude Rogers, Clarence Brush, George Rogers, John Stansbury, and Harold Greene. (Huntington High School.)

The 1944–1945 Garden City boys' basketball team featured Carl Braun (holding ball). Braun played at Colgate University and then in the NBA with the New York Knicks for 12 seasons and the Boston Celtics for 1. He played in five NBA All-Star Games and scored 10,625 points. During the 1960 and 1961 seasons, he served as a player-coach and tallied a 40-87 record. In high school during the 1944–1945 season, he scored 393 points, a Long Island record at the time. (Jack White, Garden City High School.)

According to Southampton High School athletic director Darren Phillips, former Mariners girls' basketball coach Marjorie Auster was a big fighter for Title IX rights for female athletics. She led this Lady Mariners basketball team to a Suffolk County title in 1950. (Southampton High School.)

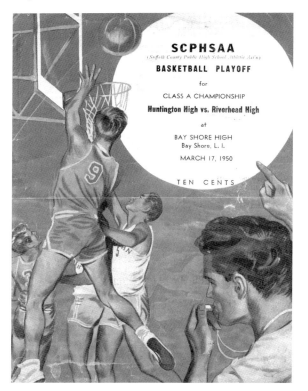

This program is from the 1950 Suffolk County Class A boys' basketball championship between Huntington and Riverhead High Schools. Huntington won the game that was held on March 17 at Bay Shore High School and featured a roster with players like John Cody, Charles Boccia, Bill Class, and Guy Rhodes. (Huntington High School.)

This program, which has a pink background and features generic basketball players, is from the 1951 Class B Suffolk County Public High School Athletic Association boys' basketball championship held at Riverhead High School. Islip was coached by Tom Veryzer, who helped the Buccaneers win their first basketball title back in 1931, while Mattituck had Robert Muir, who is Suffolk County's all-time leader in soccer wins with 509. Islip, which was 14-2 that season, beat Mattituck, which was 12-5. (Islip High School.)

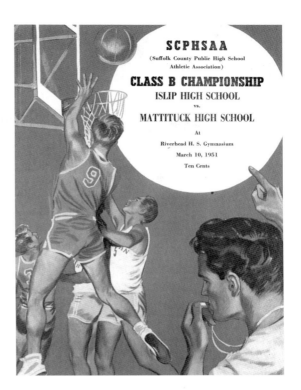

Legendary coach Carl Hansen poses with his 1953 Westhampton Beach High School boys' basketball team, holding the trophy on the right side. The trophy is not for the Suffolk County championship, because Bay Shore and Islip won the Class A and Class B titles, respectively. It is either for a league or tournament win. Westhampton had its biggest string of success on the basketball court in the late 1990s, winning back-to-back Class B New York State titles in 1997 and 1998. (Westhampton Beach High School.)

This photograph features two very famous Nassau County athletes: football hall of famer John Mackey (No. 53) as a senior and the speedster Joe Blocker (No. 30) as a sophomore. Everyone knows about Mackey's athletic ability, but Joe Blocker, who played football, basketball, and baseball, was rated as the school's all-time greatest athlete. He holds the school record for career points on the gridiron (1,433) as well as in a season (501) and game (44). Like Mackey, his football jersey number (17) is retired at Hempstead. (Albie Douglas.)

This program is from the 1960 Class B boys' basketball championship between Islip and Southold at Southampton High School. The game took place on March 11, and Southold was the clear favorite with a 16-1 record heading into the game. It was Islip, however, that won the county title. (Islip High School.)

Islip and Bridgehampton played each other in the Class B boys' basketball semifinals at Sachem High School on March 4, 1960. This program sports a generic basketball player. Islip (13-4 in the regular season) beat Bridgehampton, which was 15-1 in the regular season. (Islip High School.)

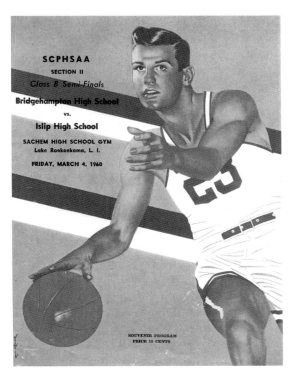

Coach Tom Bertino (left) led the 1960–1961 Hauppauge High School basketball team to a Class A Suffolk County title. Bertino was the first athletic director in school history. Marv Wietz, who coached the football team from 1960 to 1974, was an assistant with Bertino. (Hauppauge High School.)

Al Edwards

A 1972 graduate of Greenport High School, Al Edwards attended East Carolina University and graduated from there in 1977. According to the Suffolk County Sports Hall of Fame, which Edwards was inducted into in 1990, he scored 2,017 career points in high school, placing him among the all-time scorers in Suffolk County and New York State history. Edwards became a physical education teacher at his high school alma mater and began coaching the basketball team during the 1981–1982 season. He has coached the school to six Class D Suffolk County titles in his tenure. (Suffolk County Sports Hall of Fame.)

Steve Hefele graduated from East Rockaway High School in 1974 and played on Rutgers University's 1976 NCAA Final Four team, which lost to the University of Michigan. Hefele, who holds the scoring record at East Rockaway, went on to become the head basketball coach at Friends Academy in Locust Valley. (East Rockaway High School.)

Kevin Hamilton, the former North Babylon basketball wizard, averaged 20 points per game and led the Bulldogs to a 20-2 record in 1976, the same year he was selected All-Long Island. He was recruited by legendary coach Jim Valvano to play at Iona College and eventually was drafted by the Boston Celtics in 1980. (Suffolk County Sports Hall of Fame.)

A graduate of Holy Trinity High School in Hicksville, Matt Doherty played for Bob McKillop, who has been the longtime head coach at Davidson College. Doherty played at the University of North Carolina, where he eventually became the head coach. He was also the head coach at the University of Notre Dame, Florida Atlantic University, and most recently—as seen in this photograph—at Southern Methodist University. (Southern Methodist University.)

At Georgia Tech, Paul Hewitt has built a solid basketball program. The Westbury native was named Atlantic Coast Conference Coach of the Year in 2001 and has had a long coaching journey, which began at Long Island's C. W. Post, took him to the University of Southern California, Fordham University, Villanova University, and Siena College. He was the Metro Atlantic Athletic Conference Coach of the Year in 2000 while at Siena. (Georgia Tech.)

Rick Pitino spent his high school days at St. Dominic's in Oyster Bay where he captained the basketball team. From there he played at the University of Massachusetts and eventually served as the head coach at Boston University, Providence College, and the University of Kentucky, where he led the Wildcats to the 1996 NCAA title. He is most known for his long-standing position as the head coach at the University of Louisville. He briefly coached in the NBA with the New York Knicks and Boston Celtics. (University of Louisville.)

As an All-State basketball player at William Floyd High School, Melissa D'Amico was one of the best players eastern Long Island has ever had. She was a four-time All-League selection and averaged close to 20.7 points and 10 rebounds per game her senior year. She played at the University of Notre Dame, where at six foot five, she was one of the tallest girls in school history. (University of Notre Dame.)

By the time he was a senior at Greenport High School, Ryan Creighton was a household name on Long Island. He became Long Island's all-time leading scorer, passing East Hampton's Ken Wood, and led Suffolk County in scoring his senior year with an average of 26.9 points per game. Although he was a dominant physical threat because of his size and power, Creighton's legend will forever be tainted because Greenport played in Class D with less teams and lesser competition. Still, he put up points, lead his team to a Suffolk County title his senior year, and came one game short of a New York State championship. (Christopher R. Vaccaro.)

3

LACROSSE IS OUR GAME

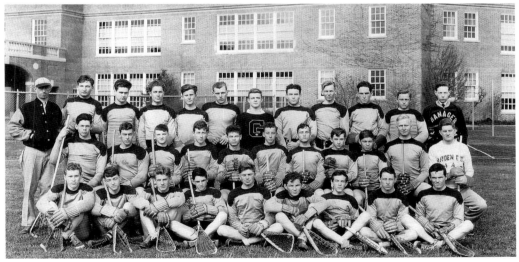

Garden City fielded its first lacrosse team in 1934, and this team shot was taken three years later during the 1937–1938 school year. Over the last 70 years, the Garden City boys' lacrosse program has built a dominant reputation as one of the best programs in the nation. It has had many legendary players and a handful of well-recognized coaches. Along with Friends Academy in 1934, Garden City's program was the second ever on Long Island. (Doug Dwyer.)

At Garden City High School, Bill Fuller lettered four times and was a Metropolitan League first-team all-star defenseman from 1944 to 1946 for a team that won championships in 1945 and 1946. He captained the football, basketball, and lacrosse teams. Fuller was a midfielder at Syracuse University and a four-time All-American. (Doug Dwyer.)

It may have plain jerseys, but the 1941 girls' lacrosse team at Friends Academy made the book because of one main component of this photograph. Many older lacrosse photographs were hard to come by, but the sport has a long history on Long Island and equipment and athletes like this are forever etched in the grain of high school sports lore. (Friends Academy.)

LACROSSE IS OUR GAME

Sewanhaka's lacrosse program started in 1938, and although it has not had success in recent years, it was one of the best teams on Long Island for a long time. This photograph is from 1955 and features legendary head coach Bill Ritch on the left side. He finished his career with a 262-54 record, and from 1948 to 1957, his teams were undefeated. He played four years at Syracuse University and is a member of the National Lacrosse Hall of Fame. (Sewanhaka High School.)

This is a vintage 1967 Huntington High School lacrosse program. The back features Blue Devils sponsors that include parents and local businesses and a brief description about the game of lacrosse. It reads, "Lacrosse is a fast and exciting outdoor team sport. Invented by the Indians living in what is now Canada, it was adopted by white settlers and later introduced into their parts of the British Commonwealth and the United States, where, with adaptations, it is played as the game we now know." (Huntington High School.)

Before James Lewis was a Top Gun graduate in the navy, he played his high school lacrosse at Uniondale where he was an attackman from 1960 to 1962. His team won 45 straight games, and he was Long Island's most outstanding player his senior season. At Navy, Lewis was a first-team All-America selection from 1964 to 1966. He helped Navy win national titles and was named national Attackman of the Year those years as well. (United States Naval Academy.)

On September 18, 1968, Raymond Enners was killed in action in Vietnam. In 1969, the Suffolk County Lacrosse Coaches Association created the Ray Enners Award, which is given to the most outstanding lacrosse player in the county every year. Enners played at Half Hollow Hills High School and later at West Point, where he supported teams in various championships. He was inducted into the National Lacrosse Hall of Fame in 2003 and the Suffolk County Sports Hall of Fame in 1991. (Suffolk County Sports Hall of Fame.)

LACROSSE IS OUR GAME

This picture of the 1960 Friends Academy girls' lacrosse team shows the older basket lacrosse sticks and the rather different form of uniform style as well as illustrating early action sports photography. (Friends Academy.)

This undated group shot from the Huntington High School lacrosse team was taken around the early 1960s. With basket-head-and-wood-shaft sticks, this group of smiling athletes probably represents the top five players on the roster. Lacrosse started in Huntington in 1957 under the instruction of Don Loughlin. The Blue Devils got their first equipment on loan from Sewanhaka High School, which had been playing the sport on the island since the mid-1930s. (Huntington High School.)

The are a few names thrown around Long Island sports history as the top in their sport on an all-time spectrum. Frank Urso is one. He is undoubtedly one of the best lacrosse players to hail from the island. Urso played at Brentwood High School, then the University of Maryland, where he would soon rise to being called one of the greatest midfielders of his era. He was an All-American for the Terrapins from 1973 to 1976 and led the school to national titles in 1973 and 1975. His 208 points rank him fourth all-time in Maryland scoring and his 32 NCAA tournament goals are still a national record. In 1981, Urso was inducted into the National Lacrosse Hall of Fame. At Brentwood, he was an All-American on the lacrosse field and was a running back on the football team that won 17 straight games while he was on the team. (Suffolk County Sports Hall of Fame.)

LACROSSE IS OUR GAME

On the left is a player from Manhasset High School, which was the first school to have lacrosse on Long Island, having adopted it in the early 1930s. The player on the right is from Elmont High School, which has not had nearly the same success as Manhasset but nevertheless had a good run in the 1970s and 1980s. Elmont won a New York State title in 1987, while Manhasset won it in 1995 and 2004. (Manhasset High School.)

A graduate of Hempstead High School, Bill Beroza is a member of the National Lacrosse Hall of Fame. He was All-Division and the team MVP at Hempstead in 1973 and as a goalie at Roanoke College was a second-team All-American in 1977. He set the NCAA record with 30 saves in a playoff game, then won six club titles with the Long Island–Hofstra Lacrosse Club. (Roanoke College.)

At Manhasset High School, John Driscoll helped the Indians win the Nassau County title in 1975 and 1976. He was Nassau County MVP those same years and was an All-American in 1976. At the University of Virginia he was an All-American in 1980 and played in the North/South Collegiate All-Star Game the same season. A member of the National Lacrosse Hall of Fame, he played for the Long Island Lacrosse Club in 1981, 1986, and 1991–1993. (University of Virginia.)

Brendan Schneck started playing lacrosse at Syosset High School. By 1978, he was a first-team All-America selection at the United States Naval Academy, then an All-American at Johns Hopkins University in 1980 and 1981. Schneck, a member of the National Lacrosse Hall of Fame, played on the U.S. team in 1982 and 1986 and won the Lt. Raymond Enners Award (presented annually by the United States Intercollegiate Lacrosse Association to the NCAA national player of the year in men's lacrosse) in 1980, as well as the McLaughlin Award (given to the midfielder of the year) in 1981. (Johns Hopkins University.)

Randy Cox was a solid wrestler at Sachem but was known for his skills on the lacrosse field. A 1980 graduate of the Black and Gold, Cox was a high school All-American and an NCAA All-American at the University of North Carolina and played for the United States' world team, winning a gold medal. (Sachem High School.)

John DeTommaso was an All-America defenseman at Farmingdale High School and a four-time All-American at Johns Hopkins University and won two national titles (1984 and 1985) at Johns Hopkins. He was the nation's outstanding defenseman in 1985, winning the Schmeisser Award. DeTommaso played on four U.S. teams (1986, 1990, 1994, and 1998) and was selected All-World. He was the head coach at Mepham High School from 1989 to 1993 and coached the Long Island Lizards to the inaugural Major League Lacrosse championship game in 2001. (Johns Hopkins University.)

Jon Reese holds Yale University records in points (200) and goals (162) and in 1990 was named NCAA Midfielder of the Year as well as Ivy League Player of the Year. Reese is a native of West Babylon and started every game in his three-year varsity football career. He was team MVP his senior season on the gridiron. (Suffolk County Sports Hall of Fame.)

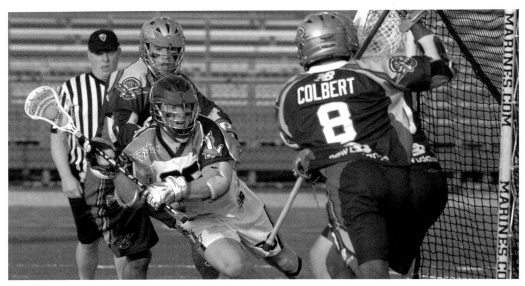

Blake Miller grew up in Manhasset, so playing lacrosse at the high school there meant good competition and great exposure. He was an All-American at Hofstra University and has played in the National Lacrosse League since 1998 with the New York Saints, New Jersey Storm, Anaheim Storm, and, most recently, New York Titans. He helped the Philadelphia Barrage win the 2004 Major League Lacrosse title and was named their Offensive Player of the Year. (Dana Kaplan Photography.)

An All-American at Oceanside High School, Nick Polanco kept to his Long Island roots by going to Hofstra University and starring on the lacrosse team there. Polanco was an All-Long Island wide receiver in high school and played for Hofstra's football team. In lacrosse, he was NCAA Player of the Year as well as the conference Defender of the Year. He has played with the New York Saints and was selected by the Bridgeport Barrage fourth overall in the 2002 Major League Lacrosse draft. In 2004, he helped lead the Barrage (who moved to Philadelphia that year) to a Major League Lacrosse title and captured Defensive Player of the Year honors. In 2005, Polanco was traded to the Long Island Lizards and won his second Defensive Player of the Year award. (Dana Kaplan Photography.)

After two seasons with the New Jersey Pride, Pete Vlahakis joined his hometown Long Island Lizards in 2006. The Shoreham Wading River High School product was a fourth-round pick by the Pride in the 2004 Major League Lacrosse draft out of Fairfield University, where he was ranked seventh in the nation with a face-off percentage of .633 in 2003. (Dana Kaplan Photography.)

In a classic showdown between two of Long Island's premier lacrosse schools in the 1990s, Sachem beat Ward Melville in the Suffolk County title game in 1993. Sachem went on to beat Farmingdale in the Long Island championship and then Fayetteville-Manlius in the Class A New York State championship. (Rick Mercurio.)

Garden City's first New York State title in boys' lacrosse came in 1994, when the Trojans beat Corning East 15-7 in the Class B championship. They also beat Stony Brook 19-4 to win the Class B Long Island title that season. Since then, Garden City has won state titles in 1997 and 2000 and is a threat to win it every season. (Doug Dwyer.)

Jay Jalbert, who went to Cold Spring Harbor High School, attended the University of Virginia and helped the Cavaliers win a national title in 1999. He has played in the National Lacrosse League and at home with the Long Island Lizards of Major League Lacrosse. He represented the United States at the World Lacrosse Championships in 2006. He was named best midfielder that season, along with capturing All-World honors. With the Lizards, he was league MVP in 2003 and helped them win the Major League Lacrosse title that same year. (Jalbert family.)

Sachem beat Port Washington 14-6 in the 1995 Class A Long Island championship to advance to the New York State tournament where the Flaming Arrows eventually lost to perennial contender West Genesee 4-3 in the final. That was Sachem's second and final trip to the state finals as a regular high school, and neither Sachem High School North or East has made it that far. (Rick Mercurio.)

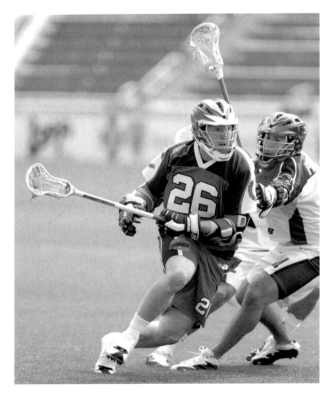

A standout on the football and lacrosse teams at Sachem High School, Doug Shanahan took his game in both sports to Hofstra University, where he was recognized with national attention on the lacrosse field. Shanahan was the inaugural Tewaaraton Trophy winner as the best collegiate lacrosse player in the country. Selected by the Bridgeport Barrage (first overall) in the 2002 Major League Lacrosse supplemental draft, he was a member of the 2004 championship team and was acquired by the Chicago Machine in the 2006 Major League Lacrosse expansion draft. (Brian Lee, Chicago Machine.)

LACROSSE IS OUR GAME

This is one of many New York State title–winning teams from Ward Melville's hallowed boys' lacrosse program. In 1997, Ward Melville, led by legendary head coach Joe Cuozzo, beat Section III's West Genesee 8-7 in overtime in the state title game and beat Hicksville 7-5 in the Class A Long Island championship. (Suffolk County Sports Hall of Fame.)

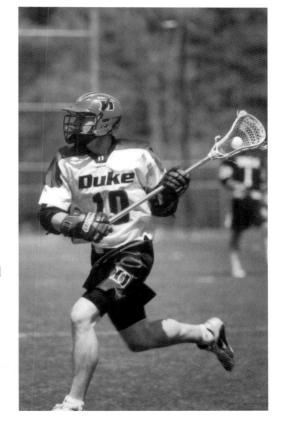

U.S. Army sergeant James J. Regan starred at Chaminade High School on the lacrosse field and then at Duke University. In February 2007, Regan was killed in Iraq. This death was a hard hit to Long Island, the lacrosse world, and everyone associated with Regan, who, according to former teammates of his, "brought every ounce of effort to his undertakings on the field and off." (Duke University.)

A 2002 Tewaaraton Trophy winner at Georgetown University, Erin Elbe had a prolific college lacrosse career. The Garden City High School graduate won multiple awards in college and helped lead the Hoyas to their first ever No. 1 ranking. In 2002, she had 81 points and was ninth in the nation with a 4.26 points per game average. (Georgetown University.)

Lauren Taylor is another Long Island product coaching at their collegiate alma mater. A standout at Manhasset on the lacrosse team, Taylor was a three-time All-America selection at Yale University and is an assistant coach there. She finished her collegiate career with 198 goals and 246 points, second all-time at Yale in both categories. (Yale University.)

At Sewanhaka High School, Tom Hayes led the school to consecutive titles from 1956 to 1958. He was an All-American at Penn State University and started coaching at the collegiate level as a freshman coach at his alma mater. Hayes was the head coach at Drexel University from 1969 to 1974 and at Rutgers University from 1975 to 2000. The Scarlet Knights were ranked in the top 20 nationally from 1975 to 1998. He was 243-162 in 32 seasons. (Rutgers University.)

John Cannella founded the lacrosse program at Lynbrook High School. His son Greg (shown here) played three seasons at Lynbrook and was one of the most prolific scorers in school history. He was a high school All-American, went to Nassau County Community College, where he was a first-team All-America selection and a junior college champion in 1985, and played in 1986–1987 at the University of Massachusetts, where he eventually became the head coach in 1994. (University of Massachusetts.)

Mac Diange is the longest-tenured assistant coach at the United States Military Academy. Diange, a product of Farmingdale High School, has been the assistant lacrosse coach at Army for more than 18 years. Prior to Army, Diange was the head coach at State University of New York (SUNY) Geneseo for nine years. He played college lacrosse at SUNY Cortland and helped the Red Dragons win a Division III national championship in 1975. At Farmingdale, he was a member of the 1971 New York State championship team. (United States Military Academy.)

At Garden City High School, Dean Gibbons set the Long Island scoring record with 101 goals in one season. He is also tied for the career goals mark (236) with Max Motschwiller, who, like Gibbons, attended Harvard University. Gibbons was an All-Nassau County quarterback on the football team, was Nassau County Player of the Year in lacrosse, and was one of the highest-rated high school recruits in the nation. He won a gold medal with Team USA at the 2008 Under-19 International Lacrosse Federation World Championship. (Doug Dwyer.)

LACROSSE IS OUR GAME

For years, John Danowski led the Hofstra University lacrosse program to big games, conference titles, and NCAA playoff bids. In 2006, he became the head coach at Duke University. Danowski, who played at East Meadow High School and Rutgers University, has earned over 240 career coaching victories. With Hofstra in 2006, he led the Pride to an NCAA single-season record 17 wins and a No. 2 ranking in the national polls. (Duke University.)

Matt Danowski, John's son, won the 2007 Tewaaraton Trophy as the most outstanding collegiate lacrosse player in the nation and was named the United States Intercollegiate Lacrosse Association Player of the Year in 2008 while at Duke. He was drafted second overall by the New Jersey Pride in the Major League Lacrosse draft. He played high school lacrosse at Farmingdale. (Duke University.)

A two-sport star in lacrosse and field hockey at Ward Melville High School, Shaylyn Blaney is one of the best recent female athletes to ever attend high school on Long Island. She was the 2007 Suffolk County Player of the Year in lacrosse and finished her career with 299 goals and 80 assists. Playing college lacrosse at the University of Notre Dame, Blaney was one of the highest-recruited high school players in the nation during her secondary school days. (Ward Melville High School.)

The Shoreham Wading River Wildcats did it again in 2008, capturing their second straight New York State Class C crown under the leadership of fifth-year head coach Bob Vlahakis. The Wildcats won their fifth straight Suffolk County title, and Shoreham Wading River became the only Suffolk County girls' lacrosse program to win a state title since the event started in 1995. (Bob Vlahakis.)

4

MAT SLAPPERS

Sprig Gardner never wrestled in high school and had brief experiences coaching the sport at East Hampton High School prior to coming to Mepham in 1936. By 1937, the school formed its first team, pictured here, comprised of 9th and 10th graders and stormed through varsity competition, taking third place in the South Shore tournament. The following year, the Pirates won the sectional championship and eventually went on a streak of 16 years with no losses. (Friends of Long Island Wrestling.)

This photograph is a unique shot of former Mepham High School wrestlers who went on to wrestle at Syracuse University. It includes Ken Hunte, who was inducted into the National Wrestling Hall of Fame in 1999, Joe Settanni, Lou Tschirhart, Hall Cook, and Pascal Perri, a notable wrestling official in America and a former Long Island champion in high school. (Friends of Long Island Wrestling.)

Wrestling at Mepham, Joe Lemyre was a Long Island champion from 1947 to 1949 and won a South Shore Athletic League and New York State Amateur Athletic Union championship in 1949. He was an Eastern Intercollegiate Wrestling Association titleholder in 1952 at Penn State University and finished third in the nation at 167 pounds in 1953. (Friends of Long Island Wrestling.)

MAT SLAPPERS

Coached by Frank Kubisa, the second coach in the history of the Huntington High School wrestling program, this 1952 group of grapplers is the typical rough and tough bunch of athletes that the Blue Devils were known for churning out every year. Kubisa had a 35-33-5 record in eight years as head coach. Lou Giani, the future hall of fame coach who would lead Huntington to national prominence, is third from the right in the bottom row. (Huntington High School.)

Johnny Harris may be Hempstead High School's best wrestler of all time. He was a two-time New York State champion at 103 pounds. He beat Carmel High School's Wayne Richards 14-4 at the 1963–1964 state tournament and Frankfort-Schuyler High School's Ernie Sportello 10-6 the year before. In 1963–1964, Harris was one of 11 Long Island wrestlers to win a state crown that season out of a possible 13. (Albie Douglas.)

Riverhead High School wrestler Joe Miles is accepting the 1963 Most Outstanding Wrestler award from Joe Valla, who coached at Amityville High School from 1947 to 1963. He compiled a 181-36-2 record in 16 years and was instrumental in the reimplementation of the Suffolk County wrestling tournament in 1949 and the start of the state tournament in 1963. (Friends of Long Island Wrestling.)

Jack Spates started his wrestling career at Smithtown High School, where he was a New York State champion in 1970, an All-American, and a four-time conference champion. He went to Slippery Rock University and won an NCAA title in 1973. In 1993, he became the head wrestling coach at the University of Oklahoma. (Friends of Long Island Wrestling.)

This is a picture of a Huntington High School wrestling team from the late 1970s. Telling from the years on the mat, the Blue Devils had been New York State champions from 1972 to 1976. Huntington has built one of the most storied and dominant high school wrestling programs in Long Island history. (Huntington High School.)

Nick Gallo started his wrestling career as a youngster in Deer Park and grew to national prominence as a national champion in the 126-pound weight class at Hofstra University in 1977. He was named Most Outstanding Wrestler that year, won a silver medal for the 1980 U.S. world team, and was presented with the Lifetime Service to Wrestling Award in 2000 by the National Wrestling Hall of Fame. (Suffolk County Sports Hall of Fame.)

A 1982 graduate of Sachem High School, Bill Starke was a New York State champion, a two-time junior national Greco-Roman champion, and a junior national freestyle runner-up. In 1982, Starke was a Wrestling USA High School All-America team selection. (Jack Mahoney.)

Freeport's Chris Edmonds (top in photograph) is the only wrestler from the University of Tennessee to win an NCAA title. By beating Hofstra University's Pete Capone in 1985 14-10 he won the 167-pound crown. He defeated the University of Oklahoma's John Laviolette in the quarterfinals and Dan Romero of Cal Poly in the semifinals. The year before he finished fourth at the tournament. (Friends of Long Island Wrestling.)

A 1992 graduate of Sachem High School, John Carvalheira was a New York State champion, a National High School Coaches Association national champion—the first from Long Island for that time—and a two-time NCAA All-American at Rider University. (Jack Mahoney.)

P. J. Gillespie left Long Beach High School as the winningest wrestler in Nassau County history with 214 career wins. He was a New York State champion his senior year and placed third in the state the three years before. He was also 41-0 his senior season and was a junior national All-American in Greco-Roman. He stayed close to home and wrestled at Hofstra University. (Hofstra University.)

The 1992 Section XI (Suffolk County) wrestling team is one of the most successful in county history. This was also a team that included many Longwood and Sachem wrestlers. From left to right are (first row) Huntington's Brian Fischenich, Sachem's John Carvalheira, Centereach's Keith Matias, Half Hollow Hills East's Jim Pascarella, and Huntington's Elias Perez; (second row) Sachem's Sean O'Hara, Rocky Point's Chad Henkin, Longwood's Duane Thompson, and Longwood's John Lange; (third row) Sachem's Jason Kraft, Rocky Point's Rob Wyllie, Longwood's Kerry McCoy, Sachem's John Aebly, and West Islip's Jason Cohen. McCoy would eventually wrestle at the Olympics, win world titles, and become a three-time NCAA All-American. (Jack Mahoney.)

MAT SLAPPERS

Considered one of the best wrestlers in Long Island history, Jesse Jantzen won an unprecedented four straight New York State titles while wrestling for Shoreham-Wading River High School. He won an NCAA Division I national championship in the 149-pound weight class as a member of Harvard University's wrestling team, becoming the school's first national champion in 66 years. (Friends of Long Island Wrestling.)

Mike Patrovich (top) was a three-time Suffolk County champion, a three-time All-State wrestler, and a New York State champion at 152 pounds in 2001. At Hofstra University, he was a two-time NCAA All-American. After college he became the head wrestling coach at Half Hollow Hills West High School. (Hofstra University.)

Mike's younger brother Ryan (left) wrestled for six years at Islip and was a five-time All-American. During his junior and senior years, he was a New York State champion, and he then attended the Ohio State University. He lasted just a semester in Buckeye land and transferred to Hofstra University, where he was ranked as one of the top 165-pound wrestlers in the Colonial Athletic Association. (Hofstra University.)

5

BASEBALL, TRACK, AND EVERYTHING ELSE

This picture is more interesting for what is written on the back. Although this is probably the oldest team shot of any high school baseball program on Long Island, the interesting facts are the names and hometowns of each player on this 1896 Friends Academy baseball squad. In no particular order, the photograph consists of Clarence Chamberlin (Floral Park), Cary Burlis (Auburn), Jacob Seaman (Cornwall), James Sliward (Jericho area), Lou Miltson (Westbury), Ed Underhill (Jericho), Ed Downing (East Norwich), Lou Rushmore (Roslyn), Will Miller (Floral Park), and Gilbert Hall. (Friends Academy.)

This well-dressed group of baseball players took the diamond for Friends Academy in 1934. From left to right are (first row) Galloway, Murchison, Kasper, Barnett, Malcolm, Eastment, Gardner, Meartting, and Paelle; (second row) M. Bales, McChesney, Reiniger, Latham, Peterson, Fergusen, and LaPierre. In recent years, the Friends Academy baseball program has churned out some successful campaigns, winning the Class C New York State title in 2004. (Friends Academy.)

This 1953 Westhampton Beach High School baseball team wore thick polyester knit uniforms, which probably were not conducive to ideal playing conditions. They are much different than the current lightweight jerseys most schools use today. Although most baseball records on Long Island do not go back to pre-1945 years, Westhampton Beach has not won a Suffolk County title on the diamond since then. (Westhampton Beach High School.)

Gerry Smith set numerous pitching records for the military service when he played during his time in the U.S. Marine Corps from 1956 to 1959. The 1950 Kings Park graduate played baseball briefly at the University of Notre Dame on scholarship and is the first person in Suffolk County history to both play and coach in a Suffolk County baseball championship. (Suffolk County Sports Hall of Fame.)

In a rare action shot from Seton Hall, Frank Barrasso receives a throw at second base to try to tag out Mercy's Dennis Smith in 1973. Mercy won 5-0 that day. Seton Hall stopped operating as a high school in 1974. (Long Island News, Town of Brookhaven.)

Ricky Caputo became just the second baseball player from Hofstra University to be selected in the Major League Baseball draft, having been picked by the Washington Nationals in the 24th round in 2006. Drafted as a third baseman, Caputo is a graduate of Miller Place High School, where he hit .444 as a senior. He was All-Suffolk that season and led Hofstra in all major offensive categories his senior season in college. (Hofstra University.)

The eclectically dressed gang is the 1899 Riverhead track-and-field team. From left to right are (first row) Leroy Byrnes, Ellis S. Duvall, Raymond H. Vail, John M. Burgess, Sydney Lash, Paul Dettner, and LeGrand Howell; (second row) Robert W. Duvall and Arther Penny; (third row) Benjamin Hallock, John Quincy Adams, Oscar Goodale, Harry Skidmore, Stanley Raynor, and Fred Seely. (Riverhead High School.)

The St. Paul's track-and-field team from 1906 was held to a high standard, according to the St. Paul's yearbook from that season. The team broke three records in 1906 and won the New York University trophy as shown in this photograph. Team captain Louis Klopsch set the school record in the 50-yard dash with a time of 54.5 seconds. (Garden City Archives.)

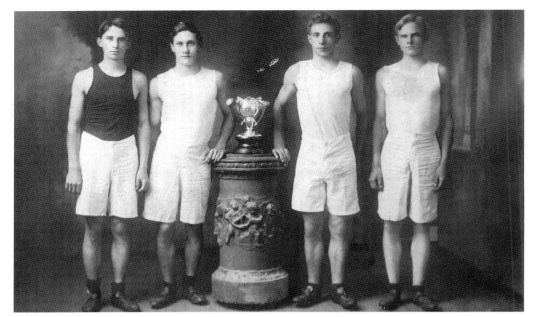

There is not much background information on this group of runners from the 1908 Southampton track team. The bottom of the original photograph mat said the four made up a relay team. It is unclear for what exact event or what their names are, and if one did not notice the spikes on their shoes, it might not even be realized it is a track photograph. (Southampton High School.)

Riverhead was well represented at the 1925 Pennsylvania Relays. At Franklin Field in Philadelphia, from left to right, Forrest A. Yeager, Walter H. "Speed" Sanford, Stanley Stawski, and C. Francis "Sam" Hallett won the Class A mile. The team was coached by L. C. "Doc" Scudder. (Riverhead High School.)

A star on the track team at Syracuse University, Ray Barbuti won two gold medals in the 1928 Olympics in Amsterdam. He was the only individual gold medalist for the United States in track and field during those Olympics, winning the 400-meter run by inches. He also anchored the 1,600-meter relay team to victory in a world-record time of 3:14.2. During his high school days at Lawrence, he won the half-mile and one-mile Long Island championships. (Patti family.)

This unique portrait of Ray Barbuti was done shortly after his gold medal–winning performance at the 1928 Olympics. The text on the portrait reads, "What a fighter this baby is! He was the only American to win a race at the 1928 Olympics. Syracuse football and track captain, who is intercollegiate 220 and 440-yd. champion and national and Olympic champion at 400 meters." It is unclear what this was used for, but it was in the possession of Frank Patti, Barbuti's son-in-law. (Patti family.)

OFFICIAL PROGRAM

SUFFOLK COUNTY CHAMPIONSHIP

TWENTY-EIGHTH ANNUAL

Track and Field Meet

HIGH SCHOOL FIELD
PATCHOGUE, LONG ISLAND

Saturday, May 18, 1929

PRICE · · FIFTEEN CENTS

This vintage track program was stashed in a small box at Southampton High School. The Suffolk County track-and-field championships were held at Patchogue High School on May 18, 1929. It was the 28th year of the annual event. This particular program lists every team relay champion from the start of the century. According to the pamphlet, Southampton won 11 county relay titles between 1900 and 1928, while Riverhead won 7 during that time span. (Southampton High School.)

As indicated in the caption of this image from 1930, Islip's boys' track-and-field team was undefeated in Class B dual meets for three straight years. The Buccaneers' only loss of the season came against Nassau County's Class A premier school, North Shore. Islip placed second in the overall Suffolk County championship with 31 points. On the bottom right is Van Wart, who had the highest amount of individual points (160) for any track athlete on Long Island that year. (Islip High School.)

BASEBALL, TRACK, AND EVERYTHING ELSE

In the 1947–1948 season, Garden City's Henry Thresher set the Long Island record in the 100-yard dash (9.6 seconds). The following season, he set the 220-yard dash record (20.9 seconds) and was the anchor on the state record–holding 880-yard relay (1:29.6). He was a New York State champion in all those events and was selected to the Look Magazine All-American team. (Jack White.)

Greg Flippen

In the early 1990s, some kids at Westhampton Beach High School did not know that their volunteer assistant track coach was one of the best track-and-field athletes ever to hail from Long Island. Greg Flippen set the New York State long jump record and won four straight state titles from 1968 to 1972 while attending Riverhead High School. (Suffolk County Sports Hall of Fame.)

William Goette was a three-time Suffolk County champion in track at Hauppauge High School. He ran hurdles in 1975 and 1976 and was selected to the Suffolk Track Coaches Association's All-County team. He was a member of the 1975 relay team that set a school record in the 600-yard dash at the New York State Relays. He went on to captain the track-and-field team at Bradley University from 1978 to 1981 and set a school record in the 60-yard high hurdles. (Hauppauge High School.)

The now defunct *Long Island News* newspaper, which covered schools in the town of Brookhaven, referred to Craig Araujo as a "running sensation." This photograph, which was taken during a League V dual meet against Port Jefferson in 1973, depicts him during his sophomore season at Longwood High School, the same year he set the school record in the mile. (Long Island News, Town of Brookhaven.)

The 1952 Westhampton Beach High School boys' track-and-field team was one of many teams coached by Carl Hansen at the school. This team captured a trophy at the Suffolk County championships and shows the growing diversity among students on the East End of Long Island during that era, which was still submerged in the civil rights movement. (Westhampton Beach High School.)

The 1957 Southampton High School boys' track-and-field team won the Suffolk County title. The group looks like it has a bunch of underclassmen and participated at a time when the Mariners were very successful at track, both at the boys' and girls' varsity levels. (Southampton High School.)

Derrick Adkins won a gold medal in the 400-meter hurdles during the 1996 Olympics. A Malverne High School graduate, Adkins finished third at the U.S. National Championships in 1991, won the World Student Games in 1991 and 1993, and won his first U.S. national title in 1994. By 1995, Adkins was a standout and won a world title. (Georgia Tech.)

A member of the cross-country and track-and-field teams at Bellport High School since her seventh-grade season, Brittany Sheffey had one of the best track careers at the school and in Suffolk County history. She helped the Clippers win conference titles from 2002 to 2006, Suffolk County titles in 2004 and 2005, and a cross-country title in 2004. A three-time All-State selection and Suffolk County Outstanding Athlete in 2004 and 2005, Sheffey accepted a scholarship to the University of Tennessee for track. (University of Tennessee.)

BASEBALL, TRACK, AND EVERYTHING ELSE

Jim Steen, pictured on the right, was Garden City's boys' soccer coach from 1933 to 1970. He compiled a 281-114-55 coaching record and won six Nassau County titles. This photograph is of Steen with his first team back in 1933. In the present day, the Jim Steen Award is given to Nassau's most outstanding soccer player every year. (Jack White.)

The 1957 Hauppauge High School soccer team was 9-4-1. For years, Hauppauge had semicompetitive teams in soccer, but nothing manifested. Then, in 1996, the Eagles won their first Class B Suffolk County title. The following year, they won the Long Island championship and repeated in 1999. Head coach John Ruffini, who took over many years after this photograph was taken, captured over 370 career victories as one of the top coaches in Long Island history. (Hauppauge High School.)

A graduate of West Islip High School, Alan Mayer is one of Long Island's top soccer players ever. He played four seasons at James Madison University and was team MVP each season. He set the school record for career and season shutouts and was drafted by the Baltimore Comets of the North American Soccer League (NASL) in 1974. By 1978, Mayer was the NASL's North American Player of the Year. (Suffolk County Sports Hall of Fame.)

Kelli Hughes became the second goalie in the country to record 1,000 or more saves at the high school level. A 2008 graduate of East Rockaway High School, she earned All-State soccer honors in 2007 and was honored as one of the top athletes in Nassau County her senior season. (East Rockaway High School.)

The St. Paul's golf team in 1900 had five members. The yearbook from that year, though, has only last names and not in any order: Hull, Mallouf, Mehl, Murphy, and Parsons, the team captain. The yearbook describes each of their golf games, especially that of Parsons, who drove "neither exceptionally well nor poorly. His mashie shots, however are excellent." (Garden City Archives.)

Surprisingly rare, this photograph is one of very few Varsity H Club pictures at any photograph archive on Long Island. Generally a varsity club consists of top athletes and team captains. In this photograph from Huntington High School taken in 1930, the boys stand and kneel in unison. The only names listed are advisor T. J. Finley, president George Gove, vice president Russell Corsa, and secretary Jack Aaronsen. (Huntington High School.)

Possibly one of the most odd photographs in the book, this 1940 Westhampton Beach High School horseshoe team is in a league of its own. There are no records of horseshoe competitions in Suffolk County, but the picture clearly shows this group of five young lads who won a county championship. (Westhampton Beach High School.)

For some reason, most early girls' athletic photographs at Westhampton Beach High School include a prop from the many sports offered at the school. It is unclear if the picture represents captains, successful athletes, or just goofiness. This group of young ladies played during the 1952 school year. (Westhampton Beach High School.)

BASEBALL, TRACK, AND EVERYTHING ELSE

This Westhampton Beach cheerleading squad is conservatively dressed with poodle skirts and sweater tops. As with just about every school in the United States, these cheerleaders came to play, cheering for the football and boys' basketball programs during 1953 season. (Westhampton Beach High School.)

This 1953 Westhampton Beach High School boys' volleyball team was coached by Carl Hansen and won the Suffolk County Class B title. Although the shiny short shorts do not do justice compared to the more modern uniforms of today, the team did have the privilege of being coached by a gentleman and legend. (Westhampton Beach High School.)

This photograph rates with the horseshoe champions photograph from Westhampton Beach and is a one-of-a-kind archery shot from the 1957 season at Friends Academy. Either it was posed or the girl on the left has a pretty good shot. That apple took a beating. This was most likely a club at the school, as it was nearly impossible to find actual Nassau or Suffolk County records of the event. (Friends Academy.)

Action sports photography was not very prevalent at the high school level in the 1960s, especially for girls' sports. That is why this shot of the 1960 Friends Academy field hockey team is all the better. It is unknown who the girls are and what school the opponent is, but it is a clear photograph of some early field hockey action on Long Island. (Friends Academy.)

At Garden City High School, she was known as Lara Von Seelen, but on television and in the present day, she is Lara Spencer. For the Trojans in 1987, Von Seelen was among New York's top divers. She graduated from Penn State University and in her professional career has served as cohost of the syndicated television newsmagazine *The Insider*, as well as *Entertainment Tonight* and *Antiques Roadshow*. (Jack White.)

St. Paul's was the first school on Long Island to have a hockey program. There have only been a handful of players who have played hockey professionally from Long Island. In this photograph from 1900 are goalie Harry Gardiner, H. J. Patton, H. F. Good, T. M. Goldsborough, T. E. Steinway, George Bissell, and W. T. Hawe. (Garden City Archives.)

Diane Nelson has over 1,000 career victories as a jockey. Nelson graduated from Sachem High School and is one of only a few regular female jockeys riding in New York. She credits Saratoga as her favorite track and began riding at age 10 on Long Island. Many consider her a hall of fame jockey and a pioneer for the success that women on horses are recognized for. (Suffolk County Sports Hall of Fame.)

BASEBALL, TRACK, AND EVERYTHING ELSE

6

LEGENDARY COACHES

Lou Howard was a fixture in Amityville from his rise as an athlete, teacher, coach, politician, and friend of many. He had a career winning percentage of .846, which is tops for anyone who coached 10 or more seasons in New York State. He was Suffolk County Coach of the Year from 1954 to 1958, and his team won the Rutgers Trophy as the best team in the country from 1954 to 1957 and 1960 to 1961. (Lou Howard.)

Former Greenport head football coach Dorrie Jackson talks with players Bill Lieblein (center) and John Moore in the 1960s. Jackson was coach for 28 seasons and compiled a record of 148-44-6, capturing 11 league titles. The football field at Greenport is named after him. (Suffolk County Sports Hall of Fame.)

Former Huntington High School football head coach Al Donofrio stands with players James Leath (left) and Bob Brush during the 1959–1960 season. Most of Huntington's success in football came in the late 1990s and early 21st century, but many former Blue Devils from the 1960s recall Donofrio as being a textbook, fundamentally sound coach. (Huntington High School.)

LEGENDARY COACHES

A native of Central Islip, George O'Leary played and coached at his alma mater. He was the head football coach at Central Islip in 1975–1976 before moving on to Liverpool High School in Upstate New York, where he stayed for five seasons. He spent time as an assistant at Syracuse University and was the head coach at Georgia Tech from 1995 to 2001. He is pictured here as the head coach at the University of Central Florida, where he was for the five years before this book was published in 2009. (University of Central Florida.)

From left to right, Doug Jones, Marv Wietz, and Bob Druckenmiller made up the 1973 football coaching staff at Hauppauge High School. Each of the men served the Hauppauge School District's athletic program for many years. Wietz is a former president of the Suffolk County Football Coaches Association. He coached varsity basketball at Ward Melville and Hauppauge and was the head football coach at Hauppauge from 1960 to 1974. (Hauppauge High School.)

After taking over an already dominant football program from Doc Dougherty, Tom Flatley built a dynasty of his own at Garden City High School. In his first year (1985), the Trojans had one of their best teams. His team recorded eight shutouts and allowed just 13 points in 10 games. They beat Mepham in the Conference II title game. He has over 200 career wins and ranks in the top 10 in all-time wins on Long Island. (Jack White.)

      LEGENDARY COACHES

Fred Fusaro was the face of Sachem football for over 30 years. He finished his legendary coaching career with 192 career wins, two Rutgers Trophies (1977 and 1986), and a Suffolk County record 22 straight playoff appearances. He retired from being a head coach at Sachem in 2003 and became an assistant at John Glenn High School under one of his former players, Dave Shanahan. (Sachem High School North.)

Bill Basel retired from coaching at Chaminade High School in 2008, after 41 years of coaching. He is shown in this photograph being hoisted by his team after the 1987 Catholic High School Football League title game. The Flyers beat St. John the Baptist 27-6 in the game. (Chaminade High School.)

Seen here is a classic Long Island sports photograph of the Cipp trio, Joe (center) with sons Jeff (left) and Joe. This shot was taken after the 2005 Class II Long Island championship. Both sons have spent many years coaching with their father at Bellport, also their alma mater. Joe III coached Longwood to a Long Island title in 1996, and Jeff was an All-American in high school before playing at the University of Kentucky and University of Maine. (Joe Cipp.)

It is never easy to form a dynasty, but William Floyd's Paul Longo did it for the Colonials. His teams won 42 straight games from 2005 to 2008. The Colonials also won three straight Long Island, Suffolk County, and Division I titles from 2005 to 2007, and many of his players went on to win high-profile awards on the island. Floyd also captured three straight Rutgers Trophies from 2005 to 2007. (Christopher R. Vaccaro.)

LEGENDARY COACHES

Longtime Huntington High School wrestling coach Lou Giani, who won the 1953 Suffolk County title as a wrestler at Huntington, won a gold medal at the 1959 Pan American Games and had several match wins at the 1960 Olympics in Rome. At Huntington, his teams have won over 100 matches, wrestlers have won more than 20 state titles, and he has the highest winning percentage in history. (Friends of Long Island Wrestling.)

Synonymous with one of Long Island's most notable tournaments for any sport, Sprig Gardner is one of the island's wrestling pioneers. At Mepham, Gardner strung together an amazing career from 1936 to 1958 at the helm of a program that won 100 straight meets, and then another 130 straight meets after that. He finished his career with a 254-5-1 record, having won 40 tournament titles and graduating 106 sectional champions in 22 years. Every year, teams from Nassau and Suffolk Counties participate in the Sprig Gardner Tournament. (Mepham High School.)

These two men have been involved with wresting for many years. Al Bevilacqua (left) was the head wrestling coach at Massapequa High School from 1962 to 1977, served two years as the head coach at Hofstra University, and was on the USA Wrestling national coaching staff from 1983 to 1991. Joe Campo was the head coach at Brentwood High School and compiled 324 dual-meet wins (part of those wins came at Section III's Frankfort-Schuyler High School). (Friends of Long Island Wrestling.)

In 33 years at the helm of Deer Park High School wrestling, Ed Luksik became a coaching legend. He coached two state title winners in Ray Downey and Angelo Zegarelli. Luksik finished his career with 233 dual-meet wins and was honored by receiving the National Wrestling Hall of Fame's Lifetime Service Award. (Friends of Long Island Wrestling.)

LEGENDARY COACHES

A member of the New York State Wrestling Hall of Fame, Tony Mellino is the former head coach of the West Islip High School wrestling program. His teams captured 312 dual-meet wins in his 32-year coaching career. He ranks in the top 30 in New York and top 3 in Suffolk County for career wins. (Friends of Long Island Wrestling.)

A member of the National Lacrosse Hall of Fame, Alan Lowe was a successful player and coach at multiple levels. At Hempstead High School, Lowe was All-Division in 1960, second-team All-County in 1961, and first-team All-County in 1962. At the University of Maryland, he won a national championship in 1967. A member of the 1974 U.S. team that won the Lacrosse World Championship, Lowe coached at Manhasset High School from 1974 to 2006, winning eight divisional titles, four Nassau County titles, two Long Island championships, and more than 500 games. (Alan Lowe.)

In Yonkers, Joe Cuozzo was not able to play high school lacrosse because his school did not offer it. At SUNY Cortland, however, he got his first taste of the game and has been in love ever since. Cuozzo is the all-time winningest high school lacrosse coach in America. With over 700 career wins, Cuozzo built a dynasty at Ward Melville High School, where he coached from 1969 to 2006. He took the head coaching job at Mount Sinai the following year and led the Mustangs to a New York State title within two seasons. Cuozzo is a member of the National Lacrosse Hall of Fame, and his teams have won more than 10 Long Island titles, 15 Suffolk County titles, and 5 state crowns. (Ward Melville High School.)

LEGENDARY COACHES

In 33 years as the head coach for Garden City boys' lacrosse, Doc Dougherty won 565 games. Garden City has long been a hotbed for lacrosse stars in America. The school has captured numerous titles and plays Manhasset High School in the Woodstick Classic every year. That rivalry, which dates back to 1935, is the oldest continual public school series in America. Dougherty also coached football at Garden City. (Jack White.)

Larry Glenz has won nearly 400 games as the head coach of the Lynbrook High School boys' lacrosse team. He is a member of the National High School Coaches Hall of Fame, the New York State High School Coaches Hall of Fame, and the Long Island Metropolitan Lacrosse Hall of Fame. He led Lynbrook to New York State titles in 1999 and 2000 and Long Island titles in 1992, 1999, and 2000. (Don Roth.)

Rick Mercurio was one of the few longtime head coaches from the unified Sachem to move over to Sachem East when it opened in 2004–2005. He finished his coaching career with 316 wins, good enough for No. 30 all-time in New York State. Sachem's premier season under Mercurio was in 1993 when the Flaming Arrows won their only state title in lacrosse. (Rick Mercurio.)

Coach Diane Chapman is a legend of her time. She has led her Garden City field hockey and girls' lacrosse teams to more than 10 New York State titles. Her teams often finish undefeated, and in 2008, the field hockey team outscored its opponents 105-4 en route to state, Long Island, and Nassau County titles, as well as a 21-0 finish. (Jack White.)

After playing high school ball at Chaminade, Bob McKillop played at East Carolina University and Hofstra University, where he was team MVP and graduated in 1972. He became a history teacher and basketball coach at Holy Trinity High School and compiled an 86-25 record before leaving to be an assistant at Davidson College in 1978. That lasted one year before McKillop moved back to Long Island to coach at Long Island Lutheran High School, leading it to five New York State titles. McKillop returned to Davidson in 1989 and has won more than 340 games. (Davidson College.)

Coach Jack Agostino has been at the helm of one of New York's greatest high school basketball dynasties and perhaps Long Island's best. At press time for this book, Agostino led Amityville High School to 4 New York State titles, 8 Long Island championships, and 10 Suffolk County crowns. He has won over 350 games and has a winning percentage of over 80 percent. He is a member of the Suffolk County Sports Hall of Fame and the New York State Basketball Hall of Fame. (Amityville High School.)

With more than 700 career coaching victories, Ed Petrie is one of the most successful high school basketball coaches in the country. Before leading East Hampton to various titles, he was the coach at Pierson High School in Sag Harbor. He played ball at Seton Hall University and was drafted by the New York Knicks in 1956. His playing career did not last long, so he went into teaching, and by 1968, he led Pierson to the school's first state title. East Hampton won a state title in 1988–1989. (Brett Mauser.)

Serving as the varsity baseball coach at Lynbrook from 1976 to 2001, Don Roth won 370 games and his teams qualified for the playoffs in 20 of his 26 seasons. His teams were four-time league champions, and he was also a four-time Coach of the Year. He has coached numerous successful ballplayers who have played in college and at the professional levels, including his son Tim, who played at Georgia Southern University and signed with the Kansas City Royals before playing one year of independent ball. (Don Roth.)

7

PROFESSIONAL ATHLETES

Ed Danowski, a Riverhead native, quarterbacked the New York Giants to the 1934 and 1936 NFL championships. After attending Riverhead High School, Danowski starred at Fordham University as an All-American in 1932 and 1933. Danowski spent eight seasons with the Giants from 1934 to 1941, made three All-Pro teams, and finished his career with 37 touchdown passes, 3,817 yards, and a 58.1 quarterback rating. He coached at Fordham from 1946 to 1954 and taught and coached in the East Meadow School District until his retirement in 1977. (Suffolk County Sports Hall of Fame.)

One of Long Island's most storied sons is also one of Major League Baseball's most outstanding players of all time. Carl "Yaz" Yastrzemski grew up in Bridgehampton and had a hall of fame career on the baseball diamond. In this photograph from 1947, Yaz is about eight years old and is a batboy sitting with the White Eagles, a potato farm team that regularly played against other Long Island regional baseball teams during the 1930s and 1940s. (Bridgehampton Historical Society.)

Yaz, who graduated from Bridgehampton High School in 1957, played briefly at the University of Notre Dame before signing with the Boston Red Sox in 1959. He made the major-league roster by 1961 and went on to have a .285 career average, 3,419 hits, 452 homers, and seven Gold Glove awards. He was the American League MVP in 1967, the same year he won the Triple Crown, and was elected to the National Baseball Hall of Fame in 1989. (Suffolk County Sports Hall of Fame.)

PROFESSIONAL ATHLETES

Jim Brown is a hall of fame football player and was voted the best to ever play the game by *Sporting News* in 2002. He is a hall of fame lacrosse player. Starring in both football and lacrosse at Manhasset (No. 11 on the top right in this photograph), Brown accepted a scholarship to play both sports at Syracuse, where he excelled even further. He was the sixth overall pick in the 1957 NFL draft by Cleveland. He won the Thorp Award at Manhasset in 1952. (Bill Cherry, Manhasset High School.)

Gerry Cooney stormed onto the professional boxing scene viciously fast in 1977. He won his first 25 fights and recorded knockout victories over Ken Norton, Ron Lyle, and Jimmy Young. Cooney, who grew up in Huntington and went to Walt Whitman High School, won two New York Golden Glove titles as an amateur. He finished his career with a 28-3 record (24 wins by knockout). (Suffolk County Sports Hall of Fame.)

A graduate of Long Beach High School in Nassau County, Larry Brown went on to be one of the most respected and successful NBA coaches of all time. He played at the University of North Carolina (as shown in this picture), then with the Akron Wingfoots of the National Alliance of Basketball Leagues. He also played for five American Basketball Association teams. Brown is also a member of the Naismith Memorial Basketball Hall of Fame and has more than 1,200 career coaching wins with seven teams. (University of North Carolina.)

John Mackey was the first tight end ever inducted in the Pro Football Hall of Fame. He was a member of the Baltimore Colts from 1963 to 1971 and was one of famed quarterback Johnny Unitas's primary receivers for a number of seasons. Mackey went to Syracuse University and played at Hempstead High School. His jersey number, 88, is retired at both institutions. (Indianapolis Colts.)

While at North Shore High School, Hank Bjorklund played football, basketball, and baseball and was instrumental in leading the Vikings to league titles in all three sports. On the football field during his senior year, Bjorklund was selected All-Long Island and the Vikings had their best season in school history with a 10-2 record. Bjorklund was the only Jets running back selected in the 1972 NFL draft. He played varsity football and baseball at Princeton University. (Hank Bjorklund.)

One of Long Island's most famous professional athletes, Julius Irving—better known as Dr. J—hails from Roosevelt. Dr. J played for the Virginia Squires of the American Basketball Association and for the New York Nets, who played on Long Island, and the Philadelphia 76ers of the NBA. He is the fifth all-time leading scorer in professional basketball history, has won a title (1983) and an MVP award (1981), and was an 11-time all-star. (University of Massachusetts.)

Clarence "Foots" Walker was the first player in Cleveland Cavaliers history to record a triple double, which he did in 1979. It was almost a decade after he graduated from Southampton High School in 1970. He attended West Georgia College and led the school to an NAIA championship in 1974. Walker was with the Cavs for six years before being traded to the New Jersey Nets and retired from basketball in 1980. (Suffolk County Sports Hall of Fame.)

At Syosset High School, Ed Newman was an All-Long Island selection in 1969 as an offensive guard and defensive tackle. He helped lead the Braves to back-to-back 7-1 records and their first league title before starring at Duke University. An All-American at Duke, Newman was selected in the sixth round of the 1973 NFL draft and spent 12 seasons with the Miami Dolphins. (Duke University.)

From 1972 to 1982, Randy Smith played in 906 consecutive games, a record since passed by A. C. Green yet still an amazing accomplishment. Smith, a Bellport High School graduate, was an All-American in basketball, soccer, and track at Buffalo State College. He set a state high jump record of six feet six at Bellport and was a seventh-round pick by the Buffalo Braves in the 1971 NBA draft. He was a two-time all-star and also played for the Cleveland Cavaliers, San Diego Clippers, and New York Knicks. (Suffolk County Sports Hall of Fame.)

Westhampton Beach is not known for its prowess on the football field, but Dan Jiggetts (right) got his start there. The former Chicago Bear was a sixth-round pick in the 1976 NFL draft and spent seven seasons in the pros as an offensive lineman. Jiggetts attended Harvard University, where he captained the school's first undisputed Ivy League title in 1975. (Suffolk County Sports Hall of Fame.)

Former Amityville head football coach Lou Howard poses with former player John Niland, who had a successful career with the NFL's Dallas Cowboys. Niland was the fifth overall pick by the Cowboys in the 1966 NFL draft and went on to play in six consecutive Pro Bowls as one of the top guards in the league. He was a 1962 graduate of Amityville High School, attended the University of Iowa, and was a member of the 1972 Cowboys team that won Super Bowl VI over the Miami Dolphins. (Lou Howard.)

This classic photograph from 1976 features future NFL player and coach Mike Tice and future college and NFL coach George O'Leary. Tice was a thin quarterback, and O'Leary was a wise and up-and-coming high school coach. Both left their marks on the game of football, and both got their starts as players at Central Islip. Tice was an All-Long Island selection in 1976. (Central Islip High School Football Booster Club.)

Paul Lankford was selected in the third round of the 1982 NFL draft (80th overall) by the Miami Dolphins and spent 12 years with the Fish. He was a running back at Farmingdale High School and a defensive back at Penn State University and in the pros. He also was a hurdler on the track-and-field team at Farmingdale. During the 1970s, Farmingdale was extremely successful on the football field, capturing four Rutgers Cups as the best team in Nassau County. (Miami Dolphins.)

Boomer Esiason was a 1979 graduate of East Islip High School. He held school passing records in yardage and touchdown passes until 2007 when Rob Calabrese broke them. He was a second-round pick out of the University of Maryland in the 1984 NFL draft by the Cincinnati Bengals and spent time with the New York Jets and Arizona Cardinals later in his career. (Suffolk County Sports Hall of Fame.)

Sachem is one of New York's biggest school districts and had one of the biggest linemen in the nation. John "Jumbo" Elliott, a 1983 graduate of Sachem, went to the University of Michigan and was later selected by the New York Giants in the second round of the 1988 NFL draft. The offensive tackle was an integral part of the Giants' Super Bowl XXV win over the Buffalo Bills. He played for the New York Jets later in his career. (Suffolk County Sports Hall of Fame.)

At Hempstead High School, former coach Bud Krumenacker would be the first to tell someone that Rob Moore did not look like a professional football player. He was a gifted athlete and solid receiver, just not for the system the Tigers ran. Moore went on to Syracuse University and was drafted by the New York Jets in 1990 (first round, 26th overall). (Syracuse University.)

At Valley Stream Central High School, Stephen Boyd helped lead the Eagles to the 1989 Nassau County Conference II championship. He starred at Boston College and was the 1994 Eastern College Athletic Conference Player of the Year. A fifth-round pick in the 1995 NFL draft, Boyd played seven seasons with the Detroit Lions and appeared in two Pro Bowls. In 2009, he was named head football coach at Chaminade High School. (Boston College.)

Former Major League Baseball star Craig Biggio is a 1984 Kings Park High School graduate. He was an All-County selection his senior year before attending Seton Hall University, where he was an All-America selection in 1987. That same year the Houston Astros made Biggio their first-round pick in the Major League Baseball draft. As a running back on the football field in high school, Biggio won the Hansen Award as Suffolk County's best football player in 1983. (Suffolk County Sports Hall of Fame.)

A Walt Whitman High School graduate, Tom Gugliotta was a first-round draft pick by the Washington Bullets in 1992. He played college ball under Jim Valvano at North Carolina State University. In the pros, he was with the Atlanta Hawks for 13 seasons, spent two years with the Minnesota Timberwolves, and had brief stints with the Boston Celtics and Phoenix Suns. (Suffolk County Sports Hall of Fame.)

Shane Olivea originally attended Long Beach High School, and upon transferring to Lawrence, former head coach Rich Mollo came back one more year in the late 1990s just to coach the future NFL player. Olivea went to the Ohio State University and was selected by the San Diego Chargers in the seventh round of the 2004 NFL draft. In high school, he won the Martone Award in 1999 as the top lineman in Nassau County. (San Diego Chargers.)

At Oceanside High School, Jay Fielder was a three-sport athlete, earning letters in football, basketball, and track. The former NFL quarterback told *ESPN the Magazine* one of his heroes growing up was Oceanside football coach Frank Luisi. After Oceanside, Fielder attended Dartmouth College, where he set school records for touchdown passes (58), passing yards (6,684), and total offense (7,249 yards). He played with Philadelphia, Minnesota, and Jacksonville in the NFL before playing with Miami from 2000 to 2004, his most successful stint as an NFL quarterback. (Miami Dolphins.)

Rob Burnett played high school football at Newfield High School in Selden and played his college ball at Syracuse University. He was a fifth-round pick in the 1990 NFL draft by the Cleveland Browns. He played with the Baltimore Ravens when the Browns were moved and spent 14 seasons in the NFL. (Baltimore Ravens.)

Melvin Fowler was a three-sport athlete at Half Hollow Hills West High School. He was a finalist for the Bob Zellner Award in 1996, given to the most outstanding lineman in Suffolk County. He was a third-round pick out of the University of Maryland (76th overall) in the 2002 NFL draft by the Cleveland Browns. In 2005, Fowler was traded to the Minnesota Vikings, and then in 2006, he signed with the Buffalo Bills as a free agent. (Buffalo Bills.)

Morlon Greenwood is one of many recent Freeport High School football players to play in the NFL. A third-round draft pick out of Syracuse University, the linebacker played originally with the Miami Dolphins but has spent the bulk of his career with the Houston Texans. Greenwood only started playing football as a junior in high school. He was an outstanding wrestler, earning All-County and All-State honors, and won the 215-pound state title his senior year. (Houston Texans.)

D'Brickashaw Ferguson is one of the most recent Long Island natives to make it professionally in sports. The New York Jets made him the fourth overall selection in the 2006 NFL draft. An offensive tackle, Ferguson played his high school ball at Freeport and college ball at the University of Virginia. In 2001, he won the Thorp Award as Nassau County's top football player. (University of Virginia.)

A 1985 graduate of Northport High School, Steve Park is one of only two NASCAR drivers to hail from Long Island. Hired by legendary race car driver Dale Earnhardt Sr. in 1996, Park was prized to be a solid competitor. He raced the No. 3 ACDelco car during the 1997 Busch Series season. By 1998, Park was racing the No. 1 Pennzoil car on the Winston Cup circuit. (J&K Auto Parts.)

Amityville High School graduate Mike James played college ball at Duquesne University, where he ranks 3rd all time in steals (201), 5th in assists (348), and 10th in points (1,411). He started his professional career in Europe, where he played in France and Austria. His first NBA experience was with the Miami Heat in 2001–2002, and he has since played for the Boston Celtics, Detroit Pistons, Milwaukee Bucks, Houston Rockets, and Toronto Raptors. (Harry Bloomberg, Duquesne University.)

As the 1995 Richard Sangler Award winner as Nassau County's outstanding boys' basketball player, Wally Szczerbiak, who graduated from Cold Spring Harbor High School, went to Miami University (Ohio). The Minnesota Timberwolves made him the sixth overall pick of the 1999 NBA draft. In high school, he competed in the 1997 Empire State Games with the Long Island team. He has played for the Boston Celtics, Seattle SuperSonics, and Cleveland Cavaliers. (Miami University.)

PROFESSIONAL ATHLETES

John Lannan grew up in Long Beach but played his high school ball at Chaminade, where he captained the team. He was selected by the Washington Nationals in the 11th round of the 2005 Major League Baseball draft out of Siena College. Lannan made his major-league debut in 2007 and has been a starting pitcher in the Nationals' rotation ever since. (Mitchell Layton, Washington Nationals.)

An unpolished lineman at Half Hollow Hills West High School, Stephen Bowen went on to play at Hofstra University and blossom into an NFL defensive end. He signed with the Dallas Cowboys as an undrafted free agent in 2006 and became a core player on their defensive line. The photograph here is of Bowen at a press conference at Hofstra in 2006 to announce his signing with Dallas. (Christopher R. Vaccaro.)

ACROSS AMERICA, PEOPLE ARE DISCOVERING SOMETHING WONDERFUL. *THEIR HERITAGE.*

Arcadia Publishing is the leading local history publisher in the United States. With more than 3,000 titles in print and hundreds of new titles released every year, Arcadia has extensive specialized experience chronicling the history of communities and celebrating America's hidden stories, bringing to life the people, places, and events from the past. To discover the history of other communities across the nation, please visit:

www.arcadiapublishing.com

Customized search tools allow you to find regional history books about the town where you grew up, the cities where your friends and family live, the town where your parents met, or even that retirement spot you've been dreaming about.